This Journal Belongs to:

_____

_____
Date

Love bears all things,
believes all things, hopes
all things, endures all
things. Love never fails.

1 Corinthians 13

Love Bears All Things Journal
©1997 The Zondervan Corporation
ISBN 0-310-97465-8

All Scripture taken from the HOLY BIBLE: NEW
INTERNATIONAL VERSION ®NIV ®(North American Edition).
Copyright ©1973, 1978, 1984 by International Bible Society.
Used by permission of Zondervan Publishing House.
All rights reserved.

The "NIV" and "New International Version" trademarks are
registered in the United States Patent and Trademark Office
by International Bible Society.

Requests for information should be addressed to:
ZondervanPublishingHouse
Grand Rapids, Michigan 49530

Editor: Joy Marple
Creative Manager: Patti Matthews
Designer: Mark Veldheer

Printed in the United States of America

Do not be anxious about anything, but in
everything, by prayer and petition, with
thanksgiving, present your requests to God.

Philippians 4:6

♥ ♥ ♥

_____

_____

_____

_____

_____

_____

_____

_____

_____

_____

_____

_____

_____

_____

_____

_____

_____

_____

_____

_____

_____

_____

_____

_____

_____

Whatever is true, whatever is noble, whatever is right, whatever is pure, whatever is lovely, whatever is admirable — think about such things.

Philippians 4:8

♥ ♥ ♥

Give thanks in all circumstances, for this is
God's will for you in Christ Jesus.

1 Thessalonians 5:18

♥ ♥ ♥

_____

Look to the LORD and his strength; seek his face always.

         1 Chronicles 16:11

Delight yourself in the LORD and he will give you the desires of your heart.

Psalm 37:4

Be still before the LORD and wait patiently for him.

Psalm 37:7

God has made everything beautiful in its time.

Ecclesiastes 3:11

♥ ♥ ♥

Let your light shine before men, that they may see your good deeds and praise your Father in heaven.

Matthew 5:16

Love always protects, always trusts, always hopes, always perseveres.

1 Corinthians 13:7

God who began a good work in you will carry it on to completion until the day of Christ Jesus.

Philippians 1:6

Humble yourselves before the Lord, and he will lift you up.

James 4:10

Love one another deeply, from the heart.

1 Peter 1:22

Cast all your anxiety on God because he cares for you.

1 Peter 5:7

♥　♥　♥

_____

_____

_____

_____

_____

_____

_____

_____

_____

_____

_____

_____

_____

_____

_____

_____

_____

_____

_____

_____

_____

_____

_____

Love the LORD your God with all your heart
and with all your soul and with all your
strength.

Deuteronomy 6:5

You are forgiving and good, O Lord,
abounding in love to all who call to you.

Psalm 86:5

♥ ♥ ♥

God alone is my rock and my salvation; he is my fortress, I will never be shaken.

Psalm 62:2

♥ ♥ ♥

_____

_____

_____

_____

_____

_____

_____

_____

_____

_____

_____

_____

_____

_____

_____

_____

_____

_____

_____

_____

_____

_____

_____

Worship the LORD with gladness; come before him with joyful songs.

Psalm 100:2

Blessed are the pure in heart, for they will see God.

Matthew 5:8

I can do everything through God who gives me strength.

Philippians 4:13

♥ ♥ ♥

_____

_____
_____
_____
_____
_____
_____
_____
_____
_____
_____
_____
_____
_____
_____
_____
_____
_____
_____
_____
_____
_____
_____
_____
_____

Bear with each other and forgive . . . as the
Lord forgave you.

Colossians 3:13

Sing psalms, hymns and spiritual songs with gratitude in your hearts to God.

Colossians 3:16

LORD, You have made known to me the path of life; you will fill me with joy in your presence.

Psalm 16:11

Commit to the LORD whatever you do, and your plans will succeed.

Proverbs 16:3

It is God who works in you to will and to act according to his good purpose.

Philippians 2:13

Just as you received Christ Jesus as Lord,
continue to live in him, . . . strengthened in the
faith, and overflowing with thankfulness.

Colossians 2:6-7

♥ ♥ ♥

Set your hearts on things above ... not on
earthly things.

Colossians 3:1-2

Fix your eyes on Jesus, the author and perfecter of your faith.

Hebrews 12:2

Come near to God and he will come near to you.

James 4:8

Live in harmony with one another; be sympathetic, love as brothers, be compassionate and humble.

1 Peter 3:8

♥ ♥ ♥

_____

Rejoice in the Lord always. I will say it again:
Rejoice!

Philippians 4:4

Take heart! Jesus has overcome the world.

John 16:33

♥ ♥ ♥

_____

_____

_____

_____

_____

_____

_____

_____

_____

_____

_____

_____

_____

_____

_____

_____

_____

_____

_____

_____

_____

_____

_____

_____

A heart at peace gives life to the body.

Proverbs 14:30

♥ ♥ ♥

_____

_____

_____

_____

_____

_____

_____

_____

_____

_____

_____

_____

_____

_____

_____

_____

_____

_____

_____

_____

_____

_____

_____

_____

_____

Trust in the LORD with all your heart and lean
not on your own understanding; in all your
ways acknowledge him, and he will make
your paths straight.

Proverbs 3:5-6

♥ ♥ ♥

_____

_____

_____

_____

_____

_____

_____

_____

_____

_____

_____

_____

_____

_____

_____

_____

_____

_____

_____

_____

_____

_____

_____

_____

Great is God's love, higher than the heavens;
His faithfulness reaches to the skies.

Psalm 108:4

The LORD is good and his love endures forever.

Psalm 100:5

O LORD, you bless the righteous; you surround them with your favor as with a shield.

Psalm 5:12

You make me glad by your deeds, O LORD; I sing for joy at the works of your hands.

Psalm 92:4

God's faithfulness continues through all generations.

Psalm 100:5

It is by grace you have been saved, through
faith—and this not from yourselves, it is the
gift of God.

Ephesians 2:8

♥ ♥ ♥

_____
_____
_____
_____
_____
_____
_____
_____
_____
_____
_____
_____
_____
_____
_____
_____
_____
_____
_____
_____
_____
_____
_____
_____

The LORD will take great delight in you, he
will quiet you with his love, he will rejoice
over you with singing.

Zephaniah 3:17

God's divine power has given us everything
we need for life and godliness.

2 Peter 1:3

♥ ♥ ♥

_____
_____
_____
_____
_____
_____
_____
_____
_____
_____
_____
_____
_____
_____
_____
_____
_____
_____
_____
_____
_____
_____
_____
_____
_____
_____

The peace of God, which transcends all
understanding, will guard your hearts and
your minds in Christ Jesus.

Philippians 4:7

As a bridegroom rejoices over his bride, so will your God rejoice over you.

Isaiah 62:5

Love rejoices with the truth.

I Corinthians 13:6

Press on toward the goal to win the prize for which God has called you heavenward in Christ Jesus.

Philippians 3:14

♥ ♥ ♥

The Lord is full of compassion and mercy.

James 5:11

The God of all grace . . . will himself restore
you and make you strong, firm and steadfast.

1 Peter 5:10

Christ Jesus is our peace.

Ephesians 2:14

Love must be sincere. Hate what is evil; cling to what is good.

Romans 12:9

♥ ♥ ♥

The wisdom that comes from heaven is pure; peace-loving, considerate, submissive, full of mercy, impartial and sincere.

James 3:17

The LORD is good to all; he has compassion on all he has made.

Psalm 145:9

♥ ♥ ♥

_____

_____

_____

_____

_____

_____

_____

_____

_____

_____

_____

_____

_____

_____

_____

_____

_____

_____

_____

_____

_____

_____

_____

Let all who take refuge in God be glad; let
them ever sing for joy.

Psalm 5:11

Because your love is better than life, O LORD;
my lips will glorify you.

Psalm 63:3

♥ ♥ ♥

_____
_____
_____
_____
_____
_____
_____
_____
_____
_____
_____
_____
_____
_____
_____
_____
_____
_____
_____
_____
_____
_____
_____
_____

Be joyful always; for this is God's will for you
in Christ Jesus.

1 Thessalonians 5:16,18

God has poured out his love into our hearts.

Romans 5:5

Be devoted to one another in brotherly love.

Romans 12:10

The LORD is compassionate and gracious, slow to anger, abounding in love.

Psalm 103:8

This is the day the LORD has made; let us rejoice and be glad in it.

Psalm 118:24

Let the heavens rejoice, let the earth be glad;
The LORD reigns!

1 Chronicles 16:31

♥ ♥ ♥

We know that in all things God works for the good of those who love him.

Romans 8:28

The LORD is faithful to all his promises and loving toward all he has made.

Psalm 145:13

♥ ♥ ♥

Be strong and courageous, for the LORD your
God will be with you wherever you go.

Joshua 1:9